NORTH AMERICAN
FOOD AND DRINK

Pam Cary

FOOD AND DRINK

British Food and Drink
Caribbean Food and Drink
Chinese Food and Drink
French Food and Drink
Greek Food and Drink
Indian Food and Drink
Italian Food and Drink

Japanese Food and Drink
Mexican Food and Drink
Middle Eastern Food and Drink
North American Food and Drink
Russian Food and Drink
South East Asian Food and Drink
Spanish Food and Drink

Picture acknowledgements

The publishers would like to thank the following for their permission to reproduce copyright pictures: Anthony Blake 33; PHOTRI *cover*, 41; Topham 13, 19, 39; Wayland Picture Library 7, 8, 15; ZEFA 6, 12, 40. **All other photographs were taken by John Wright.** All step-by-step recipe illustrations are by Juliette Nicolson. The maps on pages 5 and 11, and the illustration on page 45 are by Malcolm Walker.

Editor: Jillie Norrey

First published in 1988 by
Wayland (Publishers) Limited
61 Western Road, Hove
East Sussex BN3 1JD, England

© Copyright 1988 Wayland (Publishers) Limited

British Library Cataloguing in Publication Data

Cary, Pam
   North American food and drink. — (Food and drink).
   1. Food—Juvenile literature 2. Beverages —Juvenile literature 3. Cookery, American—Juvenile literature 4. Cookery, Canadian—Juvenile literature
   I. Title   II. Series
   641'.097   TX715

   ISBN 0–85210–027–3

Typeset by DP Press, Sevenoaks, Kent
Printed in Italy by G. Canale & C.S.p.A., Turin
Bound in France by A.G.M.

Cover *The last Thursday in November is Thanksgiving Day in the USA. It is a time when the whole family get together for roast turkey and other traditional dishes.*

Contents

North America and its people

North America lies between Europe and Asia in the western hemisphere. Europeans only learned of this vast continent a little over 450 years ago and still today it is often thought of as the 'New World'. North America covers an area of about 24 436 650 sq km including inland water. It is about 7 200 km from north to south and about 4 800 km across at its widest point. This continent is about half the size of Asia and twice as large as Europe.

The Arctic Ocean, the Atlantic Ocean (including the Gulf of Mexico and the Caribbean Sea) and the Pacific Ocean surround North America. The mainland coastline is about 88 450 km long and is broken by many bays, river mouths and gulfs. North America is made up of eleven independent countries. Unfortunately, there is not enough space in this book to talk about all eleven, only the two largest: Canada, which is part of the British Commonwealth and also

New York City has one of the most spectacular skylines of any city in the world.

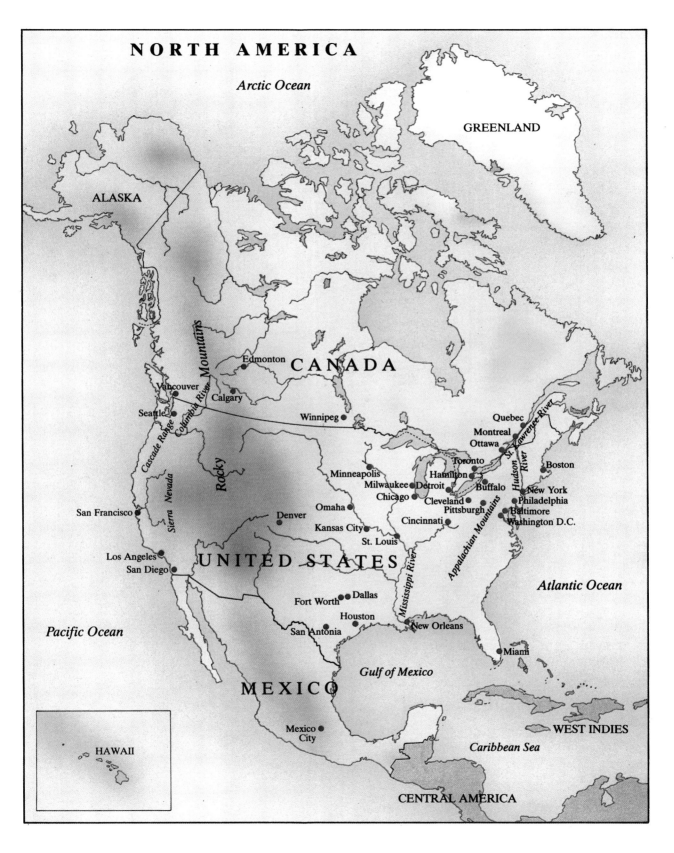

NORTH AMERICA

Arctic Ocean

GREENLAND

ALASKA

CANADA

Edmonton

Vancouver
Calgary

Seattle

Columbia River

Cascade Range

Rocky

Sierra Nevada

Winnipeg

Quebec

Montreal
Ottawa
St. Lawrence River

Toronto
Hamilton
Buffalo
Detroit
Cleveland
Boston

Minneapolis
Milwaukee
Chicago

Hudson River

New York
Philadelphia

San Francisco

Omaha

Pittsburgh

Baltimore
Washington D.C.

Denver

Kansas City

Cincinnati

Appalachian Mountains

St. Louis

Los Angeles
San Diego

UNITED STATES

Atlantic Ocean

Pacific Ocean

Fort Worth Dallas

Mississippi River

Houston

San Antonia

New Orleans

Miami

MEXICO

Gulf of Mexico

HAWAII

Mexico
City

WEST INDIES

Caribbean Sea

CENTRAL AMERICA

the second largest country in the world, and the United States of America.

Canada occupies all of North America between the United States and the North Pole and covers an area of about 9 960 554 sq km. Much of north Canada is a vast empty wilderness of forest and frozen wasteland. About 25 400 000 people live in Canada and most live within 320 km of the country's 6 400 km southern border.

The United States lies in the centre of North America and is made up of fifty states covering an area of 9 363 424 sq km. About 236 400 000 people live in the United States.

When the European Pilgrim Fathers first landed on this great continent (1620), they had little idea of the extent of their discovery. They had yet to learn of its vastness and the extent of its natural wonders. No other continent has a greater variety of resources, landscape, weather and beauty. Some of the largest snow-covered mountains in the world can be found in North America, as well as the deepest canyons, the largest freshwater lakes, the longest river system, the driest deserts, the wettest regions and the world's largest plain. Some of the world's richest agricultural land can be found in North America especially in the wide, open plains and the

The Grand Canyon in Arizona is about 451 km long and, at some points, as much as 1.6 km deep.

The dramatic Rocky Mountains in Alberta, Canada. They stretch from the Arctic to the northern border of Mexico.

prairies found at the heart of the continent. Winters are cold and summers are hot throughout most of the continent. However, the temperature does not vary much along the Pacific coast. It does not get very cold there even because of the warm ocean currents. On the north-eastern coast the climate is more severe.

Europeans brought to North America knowledge of farming, agriculture, food production and food processing. As the settlers moved across the country, they worked hard to overcome many difficulties to make the USA into one of the chief agricultural and industrial countries in the world.

Today, the USA is among the world's leading producers of wheat, oats, corn and barley. It produces enough food, industrial crops and livestock products to feed its own people and to export in large quantities around the world. Americans eat a lot of meat and a large variety of livestock, such as dairy and beef cattle, pigs and poultry, are farmed around the country. Fruits and vegetables are grown, processed and transported around the country so efficiently that families in New York can eat fresh avocados from California, fresh pineapples from Hawaii, live lobsters from Maine and fresh salmon from Canada.

7

Food — yesterday and today

It is easiest to describe the make-up of the North American population as a big melting-pot. No other continent is so mixed in race and nationality. The Native Americans and Inuit are considered the truest Americans as they lived in North America long before anyone else.

Over the centuries, people have come from far and wide to settle in North America. The first settlers were French, British and Spanish colonists who came to North America in search of free land which they could farm and from which they could prosper. Later came immigrants from eastern and southern Europe, Australia and many other countries. It is estimated that the Americans are made up of at least sixty different nationalities.

Many French and British colonists settled in Canada and today Canada still claims two official languages – French and English. Many Canadians can

The site where the first Europeans settled in Ontario has been reconstructed. Here an Algonquin Indian adds corn to a cooking pot, just as it would have been done centuries ago.

speak both languages fluently.

Since so many different nationalities and races settled across the United States, the American way of life is a mixture of European, Asiatic, Indian and African cultures that have mingled together and yet still hold on to much of their individual heritage. This is reflected in the variety of cuisine to be found in North America.

When the Pilgrim Fathers first landed in the 'New World', the Native Americans were roaming and farming a vast free land. They taught the early travellers much about survival, hunting, building homes and, most important of all, they taught them about growing food. Many foods such as corn, beans, sweet and white potatoes, maple sugar and chocolate were unknown in Europe before the sixteenth century. Yet for hundreds of years the Native Americans had been developing, cultivating, preserving and cooking these and many more delicacies for centuries. Americans today have much to thank the Native Americans for, including popular dishes such as corn pudding, popcorn, hominy grits, the corn roast and the clambake.

At first, colonists raised crops for their own use, but as settlers began to move across the continent, and different soils and climates were discovered, large farms and plantations were built to produce

The statue of the Pilgrim Fathers in Central Park, New York City commemorates the arrival of the Founding Fathers during the seventeenth century.

enough crops to sell to foreign markets as well. The south grew tobacco and cotton, the northern section of the central United States was ideal for grain crops and dairy cattle and the grasslands between the Rockies and the Sierra Nevada-Cascade mountain ranges offered excellent grazing for beef cattle and sheep. The settlers used the knowledge and experience from their homeland not only to build a better life for their families but to build the USA into a prosperous nation.

Agriculture

North America is a vast continent which is varied in climate, resources and environmental and geographical conditions. As a result, a large range of crops and types of farming exist. This chapter looks at some of the major farming areas and their produce.

Fruit and vegetables

The land along the Atlantic coast of the USA, from Massachusetts to Georgia, is poor, being either sandy or marshy. Crops such as potatoes, tomatoes, beans, peas, melons, strawberries and cranberries grow well on this thin soil helped by warm winds from the Gulf Stream. The vegetables and berries are picked quite a bit earlier than those grown further inland and so they bring higher prices in the large northern cities where there are large markets for fresh garden produce.

Along the Gulf Coast, from Georgia to Texas and including the Florida peninsula, citrus fruits and

Strawberries grown along the Atlantic coast reach the northern cities earlier than those grown inland and so fetch higher prices.

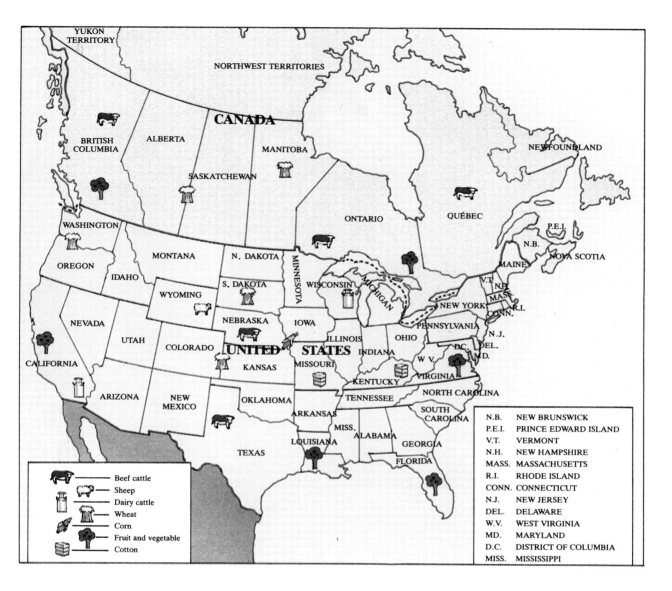

N.B.	NEW BRUNSWICK
P.E.I.	PRINCE EDWARD ISLAND
V.T.	VERMONT
N.H.	NEW HAMPSHIRE
MASS.	MASSACHUSETTS
R.I.	RHODE ISLAND
CONN.	CONNECTICUT
N.J.	NEW JERSEY
DEL.	DELAWARE
W.V.	WEST VIRGINIA
MD.	MARYLAND
D.C.	DISTRICT OF COLUMBIA
MISS.	MISSISSIPPI

Legend:
- Beef cattle
- Sheep
- Dairy cattle
- Wheat
- Corn
- Fruit and vegetable
- Cotton

This map shows the major farming areas of North America.

winter vegetables are grown. California, covering the region of the Great Central Valley and the Los Angeles Basin, has a larger variety of crops than anywhere else in the USA. Fruits, such as oranges, grapes, lemons, peaches, tomatoes and apricots as well as nuts, such as almonds and walnuts, and vege-tables, such as celery, potatoes, asparagus, onions, peas and lettuce, are all valuable crops in this region.

Inland, in the Aroostook Valley in Maine, potatoes are an important crop, and in Canada, tomatoes, corn (maize) and peas grow in southern Ontario. Fruits such as peaches and grapes grow near the Niagara Falls and in British Columbia.

Manitoba in Canada is a major wheat-growing area.

Wheat

Canada is one of the world's five leading producers of wheat which is grown in the vast, treeless plains of the prairie provinces; Manitoba, Saskatchewan and Alberta. Wheat is grown on about one out of every seven hectares of farm land.

The major spring wheat region of the USA covers North and South Dakota and parts of Montana, and produces about 30 per cent of the nation's wheat crop. The area is one of the most important spring wheat-producing regions in the world.

The winter wheat region lies in western Kansas, Oklahoma, Texas and eastern Colorado. The hot, dry summers and the mild winters are ideal for growing winter wheat which is harvested in early spring. The level land means that large agricultural machinery may be used.

Another large, wheat-growing area is in the north west, in eastern Washington and northern Oregon.

Corn (maize)

The main corn belt in the USA lies in the centre of the Interior Lowlands, and produces more than 50 per cent of the nation's corn. There is a long, warm growing season, heavy spring and summer rains, rich glacial soils and flat land ideal for using big farming equipment.

Livestock

The Interior Lowlands also raise and fatten for market more than 25 per cent of the nation's beef cattle as well as about 50 per cent of the nation's pigs.

The area which stretches from the eastern edge of the Rockies to the eastern edge of the Sierra Nevada mountains has very little rain. It is in this region that about 50 per cent of all sheep and about 25 per cent of all beef cattle in the USA are raised.

Beef cattle, poultry and pigs are

raised in Ontario, Quebec and in British Columbia in Canada.

Dairy Farming

A well-developed dairy industry has grown up in the region which stretches from Minnesota across the north east to Maine. The cool, moist summers and the marshy, glacial soils make it an important region for hay production. The large glacial lakes provide plenty of clean water for cattle which is necessary for the large dairy industry. Many large cities nearby provide markets which are very

Cowboys in Wyoming still round up the cattle in much the same way as the early pioneers of the West.

important for products, such as milk, that do not stay fresh for long.

Cotton

No chapter on North American agriculture would be complete without a mention of that important crop, cotton. The boundaries of the cotton belt depend on climate, as cotton can be grown on almost any type of soil. However, the northern boundary of the belt runs through the south of Virginia, Kentucky, Illinois, Missouri and Kansas. The cotton belt has a long, warm season that is perfect for growing cotton. The summer has plenty of rain and the drier autumn is ideal for ripening and picking.

Processing the food

All the early colonies and the first states established their own flour mills. In 1825 the Erie Canal was opened across New York State which linked the Hudson River with Lake Erie and so opened the north west to trade and industry. The new canal opened up many mills to the large wheat crops of the west. Rochester, in New York State, became the largest flour milling centre in the country. The greatest demand for flour was on the east coast where most of the people lived. As the population began to spread to the west, more and more centres for flour milling

North Americans, on the whole, eat a great deal of meat. All meat is carefully labelled and packaged under very strict hygienic conditions.

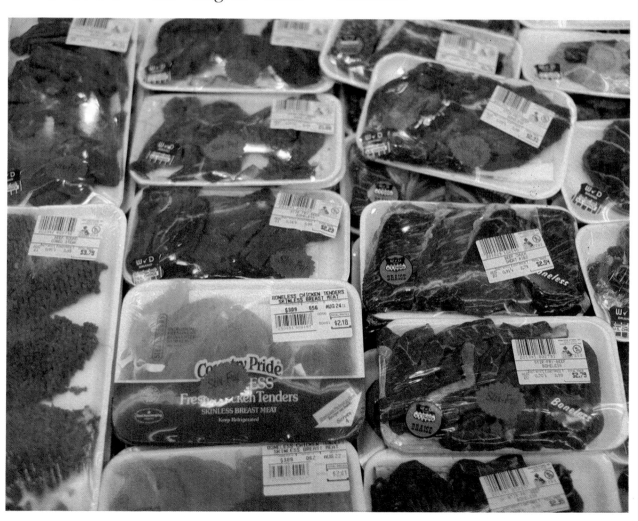

developed across the country. Today, Buffalo, New York State and Minneapolis, Minnesota are two of the greatest milling cities in the world.

In 1818 meat packing began in the United States in Cincinnati, Ohio. During the nineteenth century, refrigeration was developed. This meant that meat could be stored for longer and would not spoil during transportation. The meat-packing industry began to move westward toward cattle-raising country. Today the most important centres for meat packing include Chicago, Illinois; Kansas City, Missouri; Omaha, Nebraska; Denver, Colorado and Fort Worth, Texas. Meat-canning factories are also found all over the USA but famous canning centres include Brooklyn, New York; Camden, New Jersey; Grand Rapids, Michigan; and Sacramento, California. Meat slaughtering and packing is also a leading industry in Canada.

Fruit and vegetable canning is a very large and important industry. Canning factories can be found all over the USA. Most are found close to the areas where fruits and vegetables are grown, such as California and Hawaii. Salmon caught along the Pacific coast are mostly canned in Seattle, Washington, although many fish-canning and freezing factories can be found along the coast preparing the salmon for markets around the

A lobster fisherman in Nova Scotia, Canada. Only lobsters over a certain weight (and therefore over a certain age) may be caught.

world. Canada is one of the world's top ten fish-producing countries. Fishing along the Atlantic coast of Newfoundland and Nova Scotia is Canada's oldest industry. Cod and haddock are the chief fish caught in

North American supermarkets always carry a wide range of dairy produce.

the Atlantic and lobsters are trapped in the shallower waters. Halibut, sardines, oysters, scallops and clams are also important seafoods. Baltimore, Maryland, is the chief oyster-packing centre and Biloxi, Mississippi, is a very important centre for shrimp packing.

Most raw sugar refining is carried out at the seaports around the USA where cargoes of sugar arrive, such as Brooklyn, New York; New Orleans, Louisiana; Philadelphia, Pennsylvania and San Diego, California.

Some of these cities also refine the beet and cane sugar that is produced in the United States. Freezing factories for meat, fish, fruits and vegetables can be found throughout the country but are generally found close to the supply of food. The frozen food industry is extremely important in North America.

The processing of dairy products such as butter and cheese is a leading industry in both Canada and the United States. Creameries are found in many parts of North America, especially scattered through the eastern and mid-western states such as Minnesota and Wisconsin.

Selling the food

If you walk into a giant North American supermarket you will see a larger variety of food produce under one roof than anywhere else in the world. Here the family can go and buy almost everything, from fresh vegetables and fruits, plump and gleaming, to frozen foods and complete frozen meals displayed in large freezers. In large cities, where there is less space for big supermarkets, and in small, rural towns, the small food store does still exist.

The North Americans have very high standards and are very fussy about the quality of the food they buy. The supermarket only sells the best and freshest of foods in very hygienic conditions. Americans and Canadians are becoming increasingly health conscious. All wrapped and sealed foods are clearly labelled to show their contents and ingredients, calories

This fruit and vegetable shop on Long Island, New York State, sells top-quality, fresh produce from all over the country.

and fat content and the last date for selling. Fresh meat and fish are pre-packed and refrigerated for the shoppers to select. If the exact food is not on display, the shopper may ask for whatever they want to be specially packed.

Supermarkets cater for different nationalities, religions and trends. Oriental and Jewish foods, vegetarian dishes and low-calorie menus are available. There is often a bakery selling cakes, breads and cookies baked on the spot. The smell is so good that they are hard to resist! Visiting the supermarket is made to be as easy, comfortable and enjoyable as possible for the whole family. Soft music is played inside the supermarket and there is always a car park. The temperature is carefully controlled and there is always someone to help put the shopping into large, brown bags

This Jewish pizza shop specializes in traditional Jewish foods which are also enjoyed by people of many different nationalities and religions.

and carry them to the car.

Small food shops in cities often specialize in a certain nationality or type of food. In New York, Jewish, Italian, German and Greek shops and markets can be found selling food imported from the native country. Many cities, such as Boston and Pittsburgh, have converted old buildings into food markets. They sell a variety of unusual home-made, fresh and creative foods. Some shops stay open twenty-four hours a day and sell everything from a light bulb to a frozen steak. In the big shopping malls there are many different shops all under one roof. These include food shops selling cheeses, cookies, breads and vegetarian and health foods.

Warm, freshly-baked pastries and cookies can be found in every large supermarket. The wonderful smell is hard to resist.

The meals

Breakfast

In North America, breakfast is a favourite meal. This is because there are so many different foods and dishes to choose from. It is such a popular meal that breakfast is not just served in the morning. Many restaurants and diners serve breakfast all day long. When breakfast is combined with lunch it is called brunch.

Many people living on farms enjoy a big, heavy breakfast of meat and potatoes. In the southern states, home-made biscuits and hot breads, hominy grits, ham and chicken are often served. On the other hand, some people do not eat anything for breakfast. They may

These children at summer camp are enjoying a good, healthy breakfast outside at a picnic table.

just begin the day with a cup of coffee and a glass of orange juice.

Cold cereals, such as cornflakes with milk, are very popular, especially with children. There are

Many doughnut shops are open 24 hours a day, selling doughnuts of every size and flavour imaginable.

so many different types of cereals to choose from in the supermarket it can be a bit confusing! A plate of pancakes stacked high with melted butter and maple syrup is a traditional favourite. All over America there are pancake 'houses' that serve many different varieties all day and all night. French toast, which consists of slices of bread dipped in egg and milk and then fried until crisp, is especially popular on Sundays. Two wonderful breakfast treats that originated as Dutch dishes are waffles, like pancakes but made with a waffle iron, and rich, sweet coffee cake. Slices of coffee cake are especially delicious when dipped in a cup of coffee.

Many families go out to a restaurant for breakfast. At fast-food restaurants it is possible to order quick, easy-to-eat breakfasts, such as a toasted muffin sandwich filled with a fried egg and a piece of bacon. These are very popular with people who do not have time to sit and eat. Doughnuts and coffee are another quick breakfast. Doughnut 'houses' all over North America cook many varieties on the spot and they can be eaten there or taken away.

For those who have more time to sit and eat a good breakfast, eggs are served in many different ways such as scrambled, poached, boiled or sunny-side-up, with toast or muffins, bacon, sausage and hashbrown potatoes.

Silver dollar pancakes with maple syrup

You will need:
100 g of sifted plain flour
2 teaspoons of baking powder
½ teaspoon of salt
2 tablespoons of sugar
1 egg
225 ml of milk
3 tablespoons of melted butter
maple syrup to serve

What to do:
Sift the flour into a large bowl with the baking powder, salt and sugar. In a separate bowl place the egg, milk and melted butter. (1) Beat the egg mixture together well using an electric or hand beater. Add this to the dry ingredients and beat until just mixed. Do not worry if there are a few lumps. Slowly heat a heavy-based, non-stick frying pan. To test the temperature of the pan, drop a little cold water onto the pan. The water should roll off in drops. (2) Using about 50 ml of batter for each pancake, pour carefully into the frying pan and cook until bubbles form on the surface and the edges become dry. Turn the pancake carefully and cook for another 2 minutes until just brown underneath. (3) Serve the pancakes hot, stacked and with maple syrup poured over the top. Makes 8–10 pancakes.

Lunch and brunch

Lunch in North America can be eaten as early as 10.30 am or as late as 4 pm. It is not considered the main meal of the day. Many people are very busy and do not have time to sit down to a large lunch.

Many children take a lunchbox to school. Inside, there is usually a sandwich, a piece of fruit, a piece of cake or pie or some cookies, a bag of potato chips (crisps) and a drink. Business people often grab a quick

These New York school children are enjoying a good, healthy and balanced lunch from the school cafeteria.

sandwich or hold a business meeting over lunch to save time.

The sandwich was not an American invention but it has certainly become a very important tradition for lunch. There is a huge selection of sandwich fillings that fit between different types of bread. The peanut butter and jelly (jam) sandwich, the grilled cheese sandwich, the tuna fish salad sandwich and the BLT (bacon, lettuce and tomato) sandwich are just a few. Americans and Canadians love big sandwiches with plenty of filling. Many restaurants and delicatessens specialize in their own varieties.

In cities such as New York, business people can 'grab' a quick snack lunch on any street corner.

The take-out and fast-food restaurants are very convenient for lunch. Hot dogs and hamburgers with French fries (chips) and a thick milkshake can be ordered to take away. Pizzas can be ordered over the telephone to be picked up or delivered in cardboard boxes. For the healthier and diet-conscious lunch eaters, salad bars are very popular. Here you can serve yourself as much salad as you like for a set price! Other fast-food restaurants serve grilled and fried chicken, baked potatoes, Mexican food, Oriental food and so on. It is safe to say that whatever you want to eat for lunch, you can! Brunch has already been mentioned as a combination of breakfast and lunch. This is a very popular meal especially on Sunday after church or after a lie-in. Brunch is usually served between 12 pm and 2 pm. Many families go for brunch to a special restaurant where a wide selection of dishes are served buffet-style. Customers can go up and serve themselves as much as they like, from bacon and eggs to steak and salad. Many families serve brunch at home and invite friends to join them. Sometimes the guests are each asked to bring a dish of food which they have prepared themselves.

Egg salad and lettuce on sesame seed rolls

You will need:

50 g of mayonnaise
2 tablespoons of finely-chopped, sweet gherkins
2 tablespoons of finely-chopped onion
2 tablespoons of finely-chopped, fresh parsley
½ teaspoon of salt
½ teaspoon of mustard
½ teaspoon of black pepper
6 hard-boiled eggs
crisp lettuce
4 large sesame seed rolls
butter for spreading

What to do:

(1) In a bowl, mix together the mayonnaise, chopped gherkins, chopped onion, chopped parsley, salt, mustard and pepper. Peel away the shell from the hard-boiled eggs and place the eggs in a separate bowl. (2) Using a knife and fork, chop the eggs into little pieces. Add the chopped egg to the mayonnaise mixture and mix together well.

Wash the lettuce under cold water and shake well to remove any excess water. Cut each roll across horizontally and spread each side with a little butter. (3) On the bottom half of each roll place a piece of crisp lettuce. Divide the egg mixture and top each lettuce leaf. (4) Spread the egg evenly and place the top half of the roll on top to form a sandwich. Serves 4.

Dinner

Dinner at home in North America is served earlier than in Europe, usually between 5 pm and 6 pm. If families go out to a restaurant for dinner, they may eat later. Dinner is usually the main meal of the day when families can sit down at home and eat together. Many families also go out to dinner because it can be inexpensive and very convenient. All fast-food restaurants and take-aways are open for dinner too. In fact they are open all day long and well into the night.

The family eating at home may have a convenience meal from the supermarket or a prepared meal, such as chicken casserole or pot roast. Convenience meals are already prepared and often frozen.

Every supermarket sells convenience foods for those who do not have time to cook. Frozen pizzas are especially popular.

Many North American families own microwave ovens and this means that meals can be cooked or heated through very quickly. Microwave ovens are very useful, especially in families where both parents work.

The North Americans on the whole eat a great deal of meat, dairy products, eggs and sugar. A big grilled steak with baked potato topped with lots of butter and sour cream and a crisp salad is a very popular main meal. 'Surf and turf', as it is known in certain parts of the country, is also a favourite. This is a grilled steak served with a lobster tail. Many people enjoy Italian food for dinner, such as a big plate of *spaghetti bolognaise* or *lasagne*, or 'Tex-Mex' dishes (see page 34), such as a bowl of hot *chilli con carne*.

Different areas in North America have different dinner favourites. For example, boiled dinner with corned beef is loved in New England and the southern states enjoy glazed, baked ham or southern-fried chicken. In the mainly French-speaking city of Quebec in Canada, the tasty meat pie *tourtière* has been popular for centuries. Favourite American foods are described in a later chapter.

The people of North America love to eat informally, even at dinner. Barbecues are very popular, especially during the warm summers. Hot dogs,

Barbecues are a true American tradition. This cook is preparing juicy spareribs.

hamburgers, chicken and steaks are cooked over the hot coals and served with baked potatoes, salads and bread.

The highlight of any dinner is dessert. Sweets, such as juicy fruit pies, rich cakes with creamy icing, ice cream or cheesecake are usually on the menu, whether at home or in a restaurant.

Tourtière

You will need:

450 g of lean pork, minced
450 g of veal, minced
50 g of butter
1 medium-sized onion, finely chopped
1 clove of garlic, crushed
½ teaspoon of dried thyme
½ teaspoon of dried sage
¼ teaspoon of dry mustard
¼ teaspoon of ground cloves
1 medium-sized potato, cooked and mashed
450 g of prepared short-crust pastry
seasoning

What to do:

Preheat the oven to 190°C/375°F/Gas Mark 5. In a heavy-based frying pan, melt the butter and gently cook the onion and garlic until soft but not brown. (1) Add the meat to the pan and continue to cook, stirring, for about 5 minutes. Add the seasoning, thyme, sage, mustard and cloves and stir well. Remove the pan from the heat and mix in the mashed potato.

Using a rolling pin, roll out the pastry into two round shapes to fit a deep 18cm pie tin. Place one pastry round into the tin and press well into the edges. (2) With a sharp knife, trim the pastry around the edge of the tin. (3) Spoon in the meat mixture and place the second pastry round on top. Dampen the edges of the pastry with a little water and press the pastry edges together and crimp the edges. (4) Using a sharp knife make a few cuts in the top of the pie to allow the steam to escape.

Cook the pie for 45 minutes or until the crust is golden. Serve hot or cold.

The snack

North Americans love eating snacks and like to be able to pick up and eat whatever they want, whenever they want. From a small cookie to a big juicy hamburger, Americans love to snack! Children

Here's a young American boy enjoying a very popular snack – an ice-cream cone. It's so large he needs a spoon!

arrive home from school, or a game of sports, hungry and will often have a sandwich or cookies with a tall glass of milk. Adults often 'raid the refrigerator' late at night while watching television and finish the leftovers from dinner!

Packaged foods, such as brownies, cookies, doughnuts or cakes can be bought and eaten straight from the packet. Shops open twenty-four hours a day sell foods from chewing gum to frozen pizzas. Take-away restaurants and fast-food restaurants sell hot snack foods, and vendors on the street corners sell hot dogs and pretzels. Ice-cream parlours offer hundreds of different flavours of ice-cream that can be eaten in a crisp cone or in a small carton. Tall, hot-fudge sundaes, slices of cheesecake, pies, cakes and tarts can be bought fresh or pre-packaged. Candies and chocolate bars are available everywhere and come in hundreds of varieties.

Popcorn is one of North America's favourite snacks. It has come a long way since it was first introduced to the Pilgrim Fathers by the Native Americans in the seventeenth century. Today, popcorn can be eaten hot with melted butter or sweetened with caramel. It is a very popular snack while watching a film at home or in the cinema. Potato chips were invented in America during the nineteenth century. The potato chip has grown into America's most popular

When the Native Americans first introduced popcorn to the pilgrims during the seventeenth century, they had no idea how popular it would become.

between-meal snack. Chips come in many different sizes, shapes, colours and flavours. Chocolate brownies and toll-house chocolate chip cookies are North American traditions. The best are home-made and eaten straight out of the oven. Many businesses have grown and prospered by producing their own special recipe and selling cookies 'just like mother makes'!

Chocolate brownies

You will need:
50 g of sifted plain flour
a pinch of baking powder
a pinch of salt
225 g of butter, softened
200 g of sugar
2 eggs
50 g of unsweetened dark chocolate,
    melted
½ teaspoon of vanilla essence
100 g of chopped walnuts

What to do:
Preheat the oven to 165°C/325°F/Gas Mark 3. Lightly grease a 20 × 20 cm baking tin. In a large bowl sift together the flour, baking powder and salt. (1) In another smaller bowl, using an electric or hand mixer, beat together the butter and sugar until the mixture is light and fluffy. Add one egg at a time and continue beating until the mixture is very light. Beat in the melted chocolate and vanilla essence. (2) Using a wooden spoon, stir in the flour mixture and the walnuts. (3) Spoon the mixture into the prepared tin and spread the top evenly with a knife. Bake for 30 minutes or until a cake tester inserted into the middle of the cake comes out clean. (4) Allow the brownies to cool for 10 minutes, then cut into squares. Leave to cool completely in the tin.

Safety note:
Ask an adult to melt the chocolate for you as this needs to be done over boiling water.

Eating Out

The North Americans love to eat out. There are many different types of restaurants serving many different types of food all day, and often all night. It is possible to eat a typical breakfast of bacon, eggs, sausage and a hot buttered muffin at 5 pm!

Whether the family eats out at a small diner or roadside café, or at a sophisticated city restaurant, the food and the service are of a very high standard. Those who go out for breakfast may either sit down to be served from a long menu, or they can pick up a ready-prepared breakfast in a box to eat on the way to work. At many fast-food restaurants the customer does not even have to leave the car. Food can be ordered through a microphone and served through the car window. This is called a drive-in.

Many restaurants attract customers by showing the food being prepared. This is very popular with children. Pizza restaurants often show the cook tossing the dough into a very large, thin circle before placing it in the pizza pan. Japanese *sushi* bars have become very popular in the USA in recent years. This is the Japanese food art of preparing and eating raw fish.

This drive-in restaurant in Oklahoma City has waitresses on roller skates serving food right to the car!

Often the chef will prepare each dish and serve it to the customer himself. It is very delicious although many people do not like the idea of eating raw fish. Some seafood restaurants allow the customers to choose their meal, such as lobster, while it is still swimming live in a large tank. The lobsters have their claws tied so they cannot pinch. Salad bars are very popular when eating out. They are ideal for people with a large appetite because they can eat as much as they like.

In many cities in North America it is possible to pick a different restaurant serving a different nationality of food every day of the week; Italian, French, Jewish, Chinese or Russian, just to name a few. Some restaurants are proud to serve good home-made dishes. Some have very limited menus, such as soup and salad. Many families eat out often to save the trouble of cooking and washing-up at home.

China Town in San Francisco, California, is a very popular and exciting tourist attraction in the USA.

Favourite North American foods

Many people believe that there is no such thing as genuine North American food. It is true to say that many of the traditions and favourites found around the country are foods that originated in Europe and other parts of the world. The best of American food is a combination of cultures and traditions. The variety of favourite foods is so great it would be impossible to include them all. Many of the nationally popular foods have already been mentioned in the previous chapters, but there are a lot more.

In New York, the bagel, a Jewish delicacy, is world famous. This doughnut-shaped bread with a hole is made in different flavours and can be eaten in many different ways. It is especially delicious spread with cream cheese and topped with slices of smoked salmon. In Massachusetts, Maine and Vermont, seafood and shellfish caught off the Atlantic coast have always been a staple part of the diet. Boiled lobsters, thick fish stews and creamy clam chowders are also enjoyed by the Canadian neighbours to the north. Other dishes such as Boston baked beans, the clambake and pumpkin pie are traditions passed down from the Native Americans. If we go further south to Florida we will find a delicious dessert that originated in

Cajun cooking is one of the most delicious cuisines of North America. It is famous all over the world for its unique flavour.

Key West, called Key lime pie. In the deep south we will find Cajun and Creole cooking. These delicious cuisines combine the traditions of France, Spain, Africa and India. Many people flock to New Orleans in Louisiana to taste the very best spicy seafood dishes such as *gumbo*, a seafood soup, and *jambalaya*, a richly-seasoned rice dish cooked with seafood, meat, chicken or sausage. The deep south is also famous for homemade foods

On the hot streets of New York City it is refreshing to stop for a 'shake', a favourite North American drink.

such as pecan pie, strawberry shortcake, corn bread and honey-baked ham.

Spicy foods of Spanish, Oriental and Mexican influence are popular all over North America, especially in the south west. *Tortillas* and *tacos* are spicy meat and vegetables encased in a soft or crunchy corn-type pancake. Hot chilli and peppers, beans, fruits and vegetables make up many colourful and tasty dishes. The Mexican food found in America is often known as Tex-Mex. Many people travel great distances to San Francisco in California to taste the very best in sourdough bread. In Canada, English dishes such as roast beef and Yorkshire pudding, shortbread and scones are favourites in British Columbia.

Peanut butter was invented in 1890 by a doctor in St. Louis, Missouri. North Americans love peanut butter, especially in sandwiches. Deep-dish apple pie, served hot with a slice of melted cheese, originated as a colonial breakfast dish. Toll-house chocolate chip cookies were first developed in a little inn in Vermont.

Boston baked beans

You will need:

450 g of dry white haricot beans
225 g of salt belly of pork
1 medium-sized onion, peeled
4 tablespoons of sugar
50 ml of black treacle
1 teaspoon of dry mustard
½ teaspoon of salt
225 ml of hot water

What to do:

The night before cooking this dish, soak the beans (making sure the water completely covers them) for at least 8 hours. In the morning, drain the water from the beans and place the beans in a large saucepan. Cover the beans with fresh water. Bring to the boil and boil for 10 minutes or until the beans are just tender. (1) Strain the beans and allow cold water to run through.

Preheat the oven to 150°C/300°F/Gas Mark 2. Chop the salt belly of pork into cubes. (2) Place half the pork in a layer in the bottom of a large casserole. Place the whole, peeled onion on top. Add the beans to the casserole and top with the remaining pork. In a bowl mix together the sugar, treacle, mustard, salt and hot water. (3) Pour this mixture over the beans. Cover the casserole and cook in the oven for 5 hours. Add fresh hot water every so often to the beans if they look a little dry. After 5 hours, remove the lid and stir the beans well. Cook, uncovered, for a further 30–40 minutes or until the pork on the top turns brown and crisp. (4) Serve the baked beans hot or cold. Serves 6–8.

Safety note: Ask an adult to take the casserole out of the oven and to remove the lid for you.

Drinks

Most North American children drink a lot of milk. Adults enjoy a cold glass of milk too. Bottles or cartons of full-fat, skimmed and semi-skimmed milk and flavoured milks such as chocolate and strawberry can be bought in the shops or delivered to the home. In some very hot places, such as southern California, milk can be delivered in dark brown bottles. This prevents the sun from destroying the vitamin D. Other milky drinks, such as milkshakes made with ice-cream and ice-cream sodas, are so thick they have to be eaten with a spoon.

Coffee and tea are very popular drinks throughout the day. They come in many different flavours. Teas can be flavoured with orange, apple and spices and can be bought as tea leaves, in tea bags or as an instant powder. Cold coffee and tea are very refreshing on hot days. Iced tea is served with lemon. Soft drinks, such as Coca-cola, were

A cold can of Coca-cola is a welcome drink after an exhausting game of basketball.

invented in the USA. These drinks are also known as 'pop' and come in so many different varieties it can be very difficult to choose.

The age limit for drinking alcohol is different in each state in the United States. It ranges from eighteen to twenty one. Beer is a very popular drink in America for adults. There are breweries all over the country. The North American taste for beer is quite different to that in most of Europe. North Americans love their beer light, foaming and ice cold. The most popular beer is lager beer. Bourbon whiskey, which is made from maize, is still only made in its original home of Kentucky.

Wines produced in the Napa Valley in California are very good indeed and are now being exported all around the world.

Vineyards can be found all over the USA, from Long Island to the state of Washington. They produce a wide variety of wines. It is in California, however, where the climate and soil is ideal, that excellent wines are produced and sent all over the world. Today, white wine is the most popular of all alcoholic beverages to be drunk with a restaurant meal in America. Cocktails of every type, combination, size and colour are popular drinks in bars. Many places serve their own special combinations.

Egg nog

You will need:
75 g of caster sugar
a pinch of allspice
¼ teaspoon of ground cinnamon
a pinch of grated nutmeg
3 eggs, separated
450 ml of cold milk
225 ml of cold single cream
grated nutmeg to sprinkle on top

What to do:
In a small bowl mix together the sugar, allspice, cinnamon and nutmeg. Carefully separate the eggs (you may need to ask an adult to help). Place the egg whites into a large bowl and the egg yolks into a small bowl. (1) Using an electric or hand mixer, beat the egg whites until stiff and form soft peaks. Gradually beat in half of the sugar mixture until the mixture forms stiff peaks. In the small bowl beat the egg yolks until they turn yellow in colour. Gradually beat in the remaining sugar mixture until thick and smooth. (2) Using a metal spoon, fold the egg yolk mixture into the egg white mixture. Stir in the milk and cream and mix well. Cover the bowl and place in the refrigerator to chill. (3) To serve, pour the egg nog into individual glasses and sprinkle the top of each with a little grated nutmeg. Serves 12.

Festive food

There are many festive occasions throughout the year in North America. Some are customs of different nationalities and some are traditional American, or Canadian, celebrations. Whatever the occasion, there is always plenty of food.

A very important American celebration is Thanksgiving which always takes place in the United States on the last Thursday of November. Thanksgiving is a national holiday and families travel great distances to be together on this day. Thanksgiving is a tradition carried on from the early seventeenth-century colonists who sat down with the friendly Native Americans on this day to give thanks for the first successful harvest. Today the food prepared is much the same as that of the pilgrims although a bit more elaborate. Roast turkey with plenty of stuffing, cranberry sauce, sweet and white potatoes, *succotash*, hot

Thanksgiving brings all the members of a family together to enjoy a wonderful meal and to give thanks for peace, food and friends.

buttered corn bread and pumpkin or apple pie are just a few of the traditional dishes that fill a Thanksgiving table. Egg nog is a creamy rich drink made with eggs and is traditionally served at Thanksgiving and Christmas. For adults, it is often served with a dash of liquor, such as rum, and a sprinkling of nutmeg. In Canada, Thanksgiving is celebrated in much the same way but it falls on the second Monday in October.

Another very special occasion in the United States is 4 July. This is American Independence Day, celebrating the signing of the

The capital of the USA, Washington D.C., is the setting for some of the most spectacular firework displays on 4 July.

Declaration of Independence in 1776. Friends and families gather on this national holiday usually outside around a barbecue. Dishes of food of every sort are prepared in great quantity such as salads, casseroles, breads and plenty of desserts. Steaks, hamburgers and hot dogs are cooked over the barbecue and there are often music, parades and fireworks.

Canada Day, or Dominion Day, is one of Canada's most important national holidays. It is on 1 July and celebrates the day in 1867 when the provinces of Canada were united under one government. Canadians celebrate this day in much the same way as 4 July.

Halloween falls on 31 October and is a day which reminds children of ghosts, goblins and witches. American and Canadian children and adults celebrate this night with parties and special games. Children go 'trick-or-treating'. They dress up in funny costumes and go from door to door around the neighbourhood carrying big brown paper bags and shouting 'trick-or-treat'. If the house owner does not put some sweets in the paper bag, a trick will be played. Most people would rather give some sweets! Adults hold parties and play games, such as apple bobbing. Plenty of food is prepared and served buffet style. There is usually a big bowl of colourful punch which often includes alcohol.

These children, dressed up in Halloween costume, have already been out trick-or-treating. Their bags are full of sweets!

Pumpkin pie

You will need:
225 g of prepared shortcrust pastry
3 eggs
1 × 427 g can of puréed pumpkin
75 g of soft brown sugar
75 g of caster sugar
1 teaspoon of ground cinnamon
½ teaspoon of ground ginger
¼ teaspoon of grated nutmeg
a pinch of ground cloves
½ teaspoon of salt
175 ml of milk
100 ml of double cream

What to do:
Preheat the oven to 180°C/350°F/Gas Mark 4. (1) Using a rolling pin, roll out the pastry to line a 23 cm pie dish. In a large bowl, beat the eggs lightly with a fork. (2) Add the pumpkin, sugars, all the spices and the salt to the eggs. Beat together until well blended. Slowly add the milk and cream and mix together well. (3) Pour the mixture into the prepared pie dish. Bake for 60–70 minutes or until a knife inserted into the centre of the pie comes out clean. Allow the pie to cool completely on a wire rack. (4) Serve the pie cold with plenty of whipped cream.
Serves 8–10.

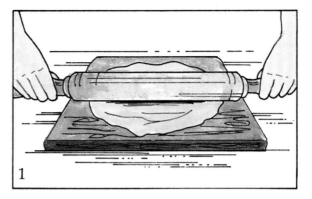

North American food abroad

Today it is cheaper, quicker and easier to cross the Atlantic than ever before. More and more people are travelling to North America, experiencing its way of life and taking back home with them many new ideas. This can be seen especially in the amount of American-style restaurants that have sprouted up all over the world. It can also be seen in the amount of American foods that are now available in the shops of many different countries.

Fast-food hamburger and pizza restaurants can be found in London, Tokyo and Sydney. Shops selling home-made cookies can be found in cities, big department stores and on railway stations around the world. Instant cake mixes can be bought in almost every supermarket. Chocolate brownies and American-style apple pie with ice-cream appear on many

A McDonald's restaurant in New York City. McDonald's, and many other North American fast-food restaurants have now become popular all over the world.

restaurant menus. Ice-cream soda fountains selling ice-cream cones, sundaes and drinks are very popular snack areas for tired shoppers in many big city shops.

Traditional North American foods are becoming popular novelties around the world. More and more people are able to order food to take away. The casual eating of hamburgers, fried chicken and pizza from a box is very popular with the whole family. Munching on a box of hot buttered popcorn while in the cinema is also a family favourite. Few people realize that when they open a bag of potato chips they are enjoying a popular snack that originated in New York in the mid-nineteenth century. Or when they bite into a

The trimmings for hot dogs vary all over North America.

hot dog, that it was a German-American in Coney Island, New York, who first introduced this way of eating a sausage just before the American Civil War (1861–5). Cereals, such as cornflakes and rice crispies, originated in North America and are now found in food shops around the world. The turkey was first found in North America and is now an English tradition at Christmas. Coca-cola and Pepsi are being bottled and drunk all over the world. As more people enjoy eating and cooking American dishes, more American cookery books are appearing on bookshelves around the world.

Appendix

North American children usually take a lunchbox with them to school. The picture below shows what such a lunchbox might contain.

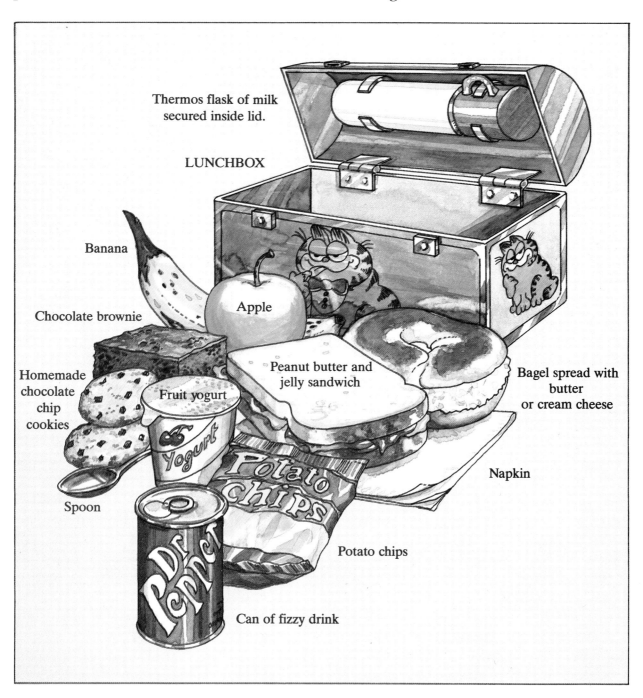

Thermos flask of milk secured inside lid.

LUNCHBOX

Banana

Chocolate brownie

Homemade chocolate chip cookies

Fruit yogurt

Apple

Peanut butter and jelly sandwich

Bagel spread with butter or cream cheese

Napkin

Spoon

Potato chips

Can of fizzy drink

Glossary

Bi-lingual A person who can speak two different languages.

Biscuits Very much like English scones and made without yeast. First made by the colonists.

Cajun and Creole Terms used for the cuisine found in the southern states of the USA. A combination of French, Spanish, African and Indian flavours.

Clambake A method of cooking seafood first introduced by the Native Americans. Seafood such as clams, oysters and lobsters are layered between wet seaweed in a shallow hole dug in the ground. At the base of the hole is a smouldering fire that cooks the seafood very slowly.

Clam chowder A thick, creamy, fish soup that originated in New England.

Colonists The people who settled in the New World when it was still a colony.

Corn bread Bread made with corn. A dish passed down from the Native Americans.

Cookie The American term for a sweet biscuit.

Diner A type of roadside cafe.

French fries The American term for potato chips.

Gumbo Spicy fish and shellfish soup from the southern states.

Hashbrown potatoes Chopped or grated potato that is fried until crisp. A favourite breakfast treat.

Hominy grits Made from ground corn which is soaked and fried. Rather bland but served with many dishes including breakfast. Originally a dish of the Pilgrim Fathers.

Ice-cream soda A cardbonated soft drink made with ice-cream.

Interior Lowlands The chief agricultural area of the United States. The region extends from the Appalachian mountains in the east to the west of the Rockies, and from southern Canada to western Tennessee, Arkansas, Kentucky and Texas.

Jambalaya A spicy rice dish cooked with meat, poultry, sausage or shellfish. Originally a dish from the southern states.

Key lime pie A rich dessert, originally using the limes from Key West in Florida.

Pecan pie Another rich dessert from the southern states made with pecan nuts.

Pennsylvania Dutch Descendants of the Dutch and German settlers in Pennsylvania.

Pilgrim Fathers The original settlers to the New World in the sixteenth century.

Popover Similar to English Yorkshire pudding.

Pot roast Meat dish that is cooked slowly for a long time.

Pretzel A savoury biscuit that is twisted before baking.

Quaker A Christian religion that was first founded in England. Many settled in Pennsylvania.

Sourdough bread A type of bread that originated in California during the days of the goldrush.

Spring wheat Wheat that is planted in the spring and harvested the following summer.

Succotash A dish made with corn and beans. Inherited from the Native Americans.

Sunny-side-up eggs Fried eggs.

Sweet potatoes Root vegetables that look like potatoes and are cooked in similar ways. They are yellow in colour and sweet.

Western hemisphere North America lies in the western hemisphere. It also includes South America.

Winter wheat Wheat that is planted in the autumn and harvested the following spring or summer.

Further reading

Brickenden, Jack, *Canada* (Wayland, 1988)

Brickenden, Jack, *We Live in Canada* (Wayland, 1984)

Cary, Pam, *The U.S.A.* (Wayland, 1988)

Catchpole, Brian, *A Map History of the U.S.* (Heinemann Educational, 1972)

Denis, Denise and Willmarth, Susan, *Black History for Beginners* (Writers and Readers Publishing, 1984)

Harris, Jeanette, *Canada* (Macdonald Educational, 1976)

Kent, Grace Teed, *100 Mexican Dishes* (Octopus, 1983)

Lomask, Martha, *American Cooking* (Octopus, 1985)

Lye, Keith, *Let's Go to America* (Franklin Watts, 1982)

Lye, Keith, *Let's Go to Canada* (Franklin Watts, 1982)

May, Robin, *Plains Indians of North America* (Wayland, 1984)

Schloret, Valerie, *United States of America* (Macdonald Educational, 1986)

For teachers:

Beacroft, B.W. and Smale, M.A., *The Making of America* (Longman, 1982)

McNaught, Kenneth, *The Pelican History of Canada* (Penguin Books, 1969)

Pierce, N.R. and Hagstrom, J., *The Book of America – Inside Fifty States Today* (W.W. Norton, 1983)

Simmons, R.C., *The American Colonies* (Longman, 1976)

Sinclair, Andrew, *A Concise History of the United States* (Lorrimer Publishing, 1984)

Index